HSUS The Humane Society of the United States

JASMINE

by Randy Houk

To Dad and Bea, with so many thanks for their faith and love.

A TRUE STORY FROM THE NORTHEAST ANIMAL SHELTER.

THE BENEFACTORY

Jasmine was a city cat –
She stayed in, and that was that.
She had water, she had kibble,
She could sip at will, or nibble.
She'd no need for kitty-sitters –
She'd just use her kitty litter.
She had learned to wait all day –
While her owners worked, she'd play.

So when they packed up and left,
Jasmine didn't feel bereft.
Often she was left alone –
Any minute, they'd be home.

But the day came shortly when
Several burly moving men
Took the tables and suitcases,
Took the books, and beds, and vases,
Took the rugs and took the drapes,
Saucers, glasses, cups and plates,

Carried off the last, large box,
Closed the door, and locked the locks.

Jasmine sat and watched the door,
Sat and watched, and watched some more.
When her folks did not appear,
She began to feel some fear.
But she had a bit more food -
Eating that restored her mood.
And she thought, with her last water,
"They'll come soon. At least, they ought'ter."

She began to prowl about.
Surely there was some way out?
Since the door was thick hard wood,
Scratching didn't do much good.
Though she looked around some more,
She could find no other door.

Jasmine tried the window last,
Pressed her nose against the glass.
No one heard her shrill 'meow,'
Not that first night, anyhow.
So she curled into a ball,
Feeling sad and feeling small.
Then she sighed, and after yawning,
Fell asleep and slept till morning.

When she woke, she noticed first,
Pangs of hunger, pangs of thirst.
She had used up all her water,
All the food her owners bought her.

She looked all around the place,
Stopping once, to clean her face.
There was not a single bite,
Not a morsel, not a mite.

And the only thing she found,
As she wandered all around,
Was a single bag of seed
For the birds her folks would feed.

Jasmine thought about the seed.
She was no bird – oh no, indeed!
But in these dire circumstances,
She thought she ought to take her chances.
Of choices she had not a lot,
So she made do with what she'd got.
She ripped the bag, and tipped the seed,
And ate a bit, and filled her need.

13

"And now," she thought, "I'd like a drink."
She jumped up to the kitchen sink,
But found the faucets were bone-dry.
No drop of water could she spy.

Next she tried the powder room,
With a growing sense of gloom.
Sure enough, the toilet lid
Stayed down, no matter what she did.

Wait. What's that? Is that a drip?
Being careful not to slip,
Jasmine jumped up to the tub,
Found a leak, and licked it up.

It took time to quench her thirst,
But no leak would have been worse.
As it was, she'd lick and stop,
Waiting for another drop.

One week went by, then another,
One week much like any other.
She ate seed, and she kept going.
Luckily, the leak kept flowing.

18

After two weeks, she grew thinner.
After six, her eyes grew dimmer.
After ten, she slept a lot,
Feeling feverish and hot.

It was Easter time before
Someone opened up the door.
Then the landlord of the place
Turned the key, poked in his face.

"Oh my gosh," he said. "A cat.
Who would do a thing like that?
You've been here for months, I'd think.
What did you eat?   What did you drink?"

Jasmine rubbed against his leg.
She didn't cry. She didn't beg.
He saw that she was awfully thin.
Her eyes were dull. She'd patchy skin.

"We've got to get you help," said he.
"You need a vet. Just come with me."

He tucked her right into his arm.
She knew he didn't mean her harm.
To a shelter he then drove her,
Where a doctor looked her over.

21

The vet said, "This is one sick cat.
What kind of people act like that?
This cat's only three pounds weight –
Exactly three, and she should weigh eight."

"I was sick," the landlord said.
"I spent three months in a hospital bed.
I lost three full months of rent
Because of the hospital time I spent.
When I got well, what did I find
But this sick cat, just left behind."

23

Jasmine looked pretty bad at that –
But purred and purred like a healthy cat.
"Can you fix her, Doc?," the landlord asked
"We'll try," said the vet. "It'll be a task."

She got a bath and she got a pill,
She got some water, and drank her fill.
They cooked for her a special diet.
Jasmine looked, and got very quiet.
She would not touch a single bite.
Not that day, and not that night.

They tried canned food. They tried dry.
Not a mouthful would she try.
They cooked fish and they cooked meat.
Not a morsel would she eat.

24

Then the vet recalled the seed.
He mixed some in with Jasmine's feed.
Up she bounced, and with a pounce,
She gulped the birdseed – every ounce.

25

Jasmine blossomed with every week.
Her fur grew shiny, soft and sleek.
She was extra friendly when
Anyone came to her pen.
Visitors came every day,
Chose a cat, and drove away.
Jasmine didn't seem to mind.
She just waited, sure she'd find
Someone special, someone rare,
Someone who would really care,
Someone who would simply never
Leave her home alone – not *ever*!

And one day, as she was snoozing,
Seven children, who were choosing,
Wanting a special, friendly cat,
Wanting a cat – well – just like that,
Scratched her ears right through the bars,
And drove her home in the family car.

Jasmine likes the number seven.
Seven children are pure heaven.
Seven children stroke and pat her.
She grows stronger. She grows fatter.
She is rarely left alone -
Someone's almost always home.

Over time, she's learned to eat
Normal food. But for a treat,
She jumps up to the feeder shelf
And eats a bit of seed herself.
For if you're a cat, and it's all you've got,
You can learn to like birdseed a lot.

If you should want a dog or kitten,
Come to a shelter. You'll be smitten.
A shelter pet makes a loving friend,
I promise you. And that's the end.

Glossary

kibble	dry cat food
nibble	eat small bites
kitty-sitters	baby-sitters for cats
litter	a tray of sand made of ground clay for cats (an indoor bathroom)
bereft	sad and feeling loss
burly	big and strong
restored	put back or fixed
prowl	search, look all over
meow	the noise a cat makes
shrill	high and loud sound
pangs	sharp pains
morsel	a little bite
dire	very bad, evil
circumstances	the way things are
quench	drown, put out a fire
landlord	the person who owns a home
vet	a doctor for animals
sleek	slippery and shiny
blossomed	flowered
rare	not found very often, special

The real Jasmine

Jasmine's family lived at a time when cars did not have seat belts in the back seat, and before car seats were invented for babies. Now the law says all children must wear seat belts in a car.

Jasmine is a true story of a cat rescued by The Northeast Animal Shelter, a no-kill shelter entirely supported by donations, at 204 Highland Ave., in Salem, Mass. Donations to The Northeast Animal Shelter are tax deductible. Purchase of this book or any product endorsed by the shelter does not constitute a donation to The Northeast Animal Shelter. For information, call: 508-745-9888.

The Humane Society of the U.S., a nonprofit organization founded in 1954, and with a constituency of over a million and a half persons, is dedicated to speaking for animals, who cannot speak for themselves. The HSUS is devoted to making the world safe for animals through legal, educational, legislative and investigative means. The HSUS believes that humans have a moral obligation to protect other species with which we share the Earth. Co-endorsement of this book does not necessarily mean The HSUS endorsement of The Northeast Animal Shelter. For information on The HSUS, call: 202 452-1100.

Text and Illustrations Copyright © 1993 by Randy Houk

Printed by Allied Printing Services
Designed by Anita Soos Design, Inc.

Published by The Benefactory, Inc.
One Post Road, Fairfield, CT 06430
The Benefactory produces books, tapes, and toys that foster animal protection and environmental preservation. Call: 203-255-7744

THE
BENEFACTORY

ISBN 1-882728-32-7
Printed in the U.S.A.
10 9 8 7 6 5 4 3 2 1